Space Launch!

Let's Explore

Uranus

Helen and David Orme

GARETH**STEVENS**
GS
PUBLISHING
A Member of the WRC Media Family of Companies

Please visit our Web site at: www.garethstevens.com
For a free color catalog describing Gareth Stevens Publishing's list
of high-quality books and multimedia programs, call
1-800-542-2595 (USA) or 1-800-387-3178 (Canada).
Gareth Stevens Publishing's fax: (414) 332-3567.

Library of Congress Cataloging-in-Publication Data

Orme, Helen.
      Let's explore Uranus / Helen and David Orme.
          p. cm. — (Space launch!)
      Includes index.
      ISBN-13: 978-0-8368-7949-0 (lib. bdg.)
      ISBN-13: 978-0-8368-8134-9 (softcover)
      1. Uranus (Planet)—Juvenile literature. I. Orme, David, 1948 Mar. 1- II. Title.
      QB681.O76   2007
      523.47—dc22   2006034867

This North American edition first published in 2007 by
Gareth Stevens Publishing
A Member of the WRC Media Family of Companies
330 West Olive Street, Suite 100
Milwaukee, Wisconsin 53212 USA

This U.S. edition copyright © 2007 by Gareth Stevens, Inc. Original edition copyright © 2006 by ticktock Entertainment
Ltd. First published in Great Britain in 2006 by ticktock Media Ltd., Unit 2, Orchard Business Centre, North Farm Road,
Tunbridge Wells, Kent, TN2 3XF, United Kingdom.

The publishers would like to thank: Sandra Voss, Tim Bones, James Powell, Indexing Specialists (UK) Ltd.

ticktock project editor: Julia Adams
ticktock project designer: Emma Randall

Gareth Stevens Editorial Direction: Mark Sachner
Gareth Stevens Editors: Carol Ryback and Barbara Kiely Miller
Gareth Stevens Art Direction: Tammy West
Gareth Stevens Designer: Dave Kowalski
Gareth Stevens Production: Jessica Yanke and Robert Kraus

Photo credits (t=top, b=bottom, c=center, l=left, r=right, bg=background)
CORBIS: Hubble Space Telescope: 17tr, 19 all; NASA: 1 all, 7tr, 7c, 7bl, 8, 13 all, 14, 15 all, 16, 20, 22 all, 23b; Science Photo Library: front cover, 4/5bg
(original), 12, 21, 23t; Shutterstock: 2/3bg, 7tl, 9b, 18b, 24bg; ticktock picture archive: 5tr, 6/7bg, 6, 9t, 10/11bg, 10, 11 all, 14/15bg, 17b, 18/19bg, 18bl,
22/23bg. Rocket drawing Dave Kowalski/ © Gareth Stevens, Inc.

Printed in Canada

1 2 3 4 5 6 7 8 9 10 10 09 08 07 06

Contents

Words in the glossary are printed in **bold** the first time they appear in the text.

Where Is Uranus?

There are eight known planets in our **solar system**. The planets travel around the Sun. Uranus is the seventh planet from the Sun.

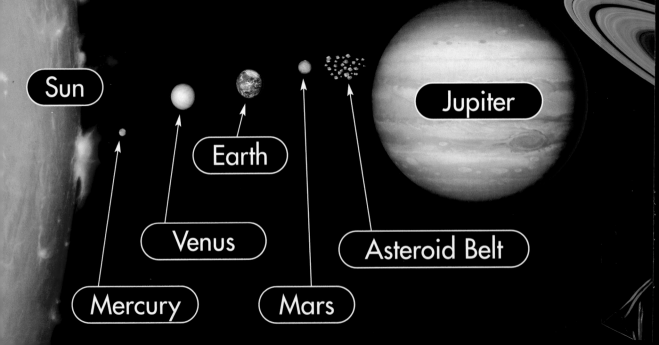

Sun

Jupiter

Earth

Venus

Asteroid Belt

Mercury

Mars

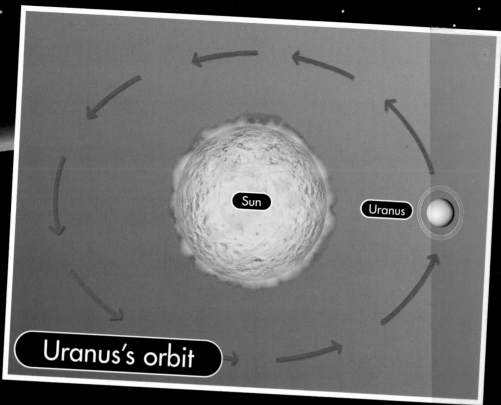

Sun

Uranus

Uranus's orbit

Uranus travels around the Sun once every 84 **Earth years**. This journey is called its **orbit**. The time it takes for a planet to travel around the Sun once is called a **year**.

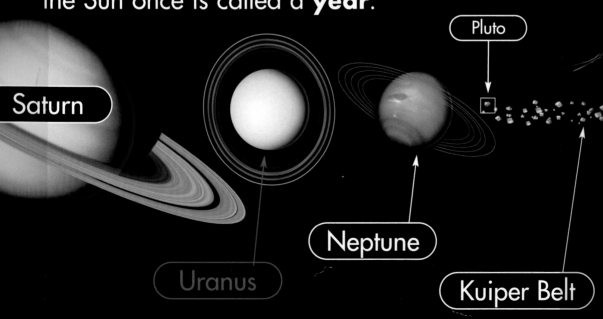

Saturn

Uranus

Neptune

Pluto

Kuiper Belt

Planet Facts

The center of Uranus is made of rock and possibly ice. Most of the rest of the planet is made up of different gases and **liquid** water.

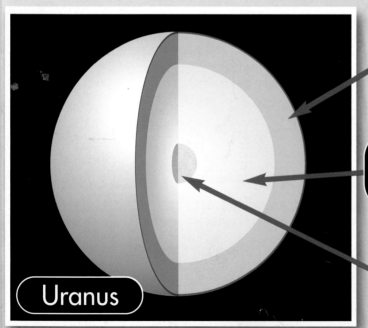

atmosphere of mixed gases

liquid water and mixed gases

rock and possibly ice

Uranus

Uranus's **atmosphere** is full of **methane gas**. It makes Uranus look blue through a **telescope**.

Earth

7,926 miles
(12,753 kilometers)

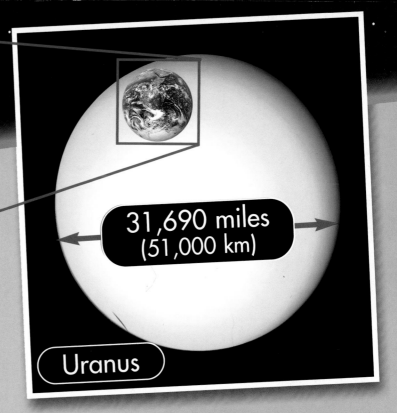

31,690 miles
(51,000 km)

Uranus

Uranus is the third biggest planet in the solar system.

Planets are always spinning. Most planets spin from left to right.

Jupiter's direction of spin

Uranus

direction of spin

Uranus is tilted. It spins sideways, from bottom to top. Some other large object traveling through the solar system probably knocked Uranus onto its side.

A day is the time it takes a planet to spin around once. Uranus spins very fast. A day on Uranus is the same as 17 1/2 hours on Earth.

What's the Weather Like?

Uranus is a very windy planet. Clouds made of a mixture of **hydrogen** and methane gases race around the planet.

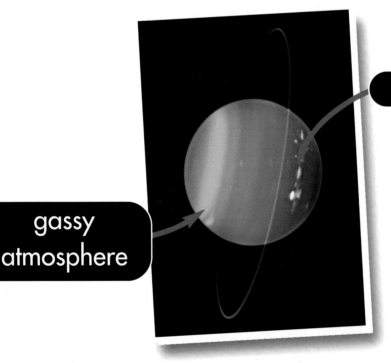

clouds

gassy atmosphere

Clouds on Uranus move at about 400 miles (644 km) per hour!

A year on Uranus lasts eighty-four Earth years. Each season lasts about twenty-one years!

but the center of the planet is very hot.

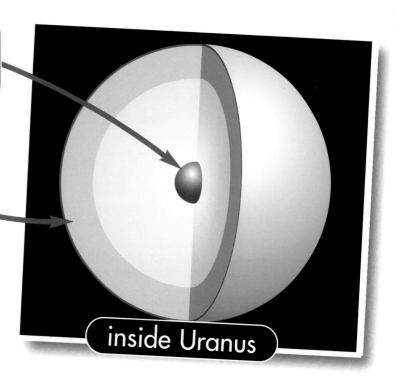

center
12,600°Fahrenheit
(7,000°Celsius)

atmosphere
-355°F (-215°C)

The lowest
temperature ever
reached on Earth
is -129°F (-89°C).

inside Uranus

Astronomers think that the atmosphere on Uranus might squeeze methane gas into tiny black diamonds.

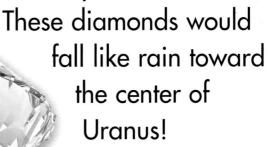

These diamonds would
fall like rain toward
the center of
Uranus!

We have known about some planets for thousands of years because we could see them in the night sky. We cannot see Uranus without a telescope.

Uranus was the first planet discovered using a telescope. English astronomer William Herschel discovered Uranus in 1781.

Herschel designed and built his own telescopes. He used this large telescope to look at Uranus.

Herschel's telescope

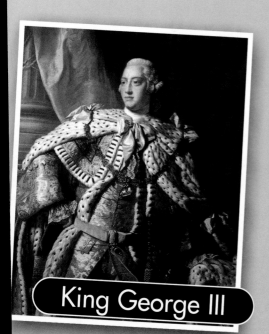

King George III

Herschel lived in Britain. He named the planet "George's Star" after the British king, George III.

The planet was later renamed after the ancient Greek god of the sky — Uranus.

Looking for Moons

Earth has only one moon. Uranus has twenty-seven moons that we know about! All of the moons are named after people in the plays of English writer William Shakespeare.

Uranus

Ariel (185

Oberon (1787)

Titania (1787)

Miranda (1948)

Umbriel (1948)

This painting shows Uranus's five biggest moons and the year they were discovered. These moons were first seen through telescopes.

In 1986, the **space probe** *Voyager 2* discovered ten smaller moons.

Voyager 2

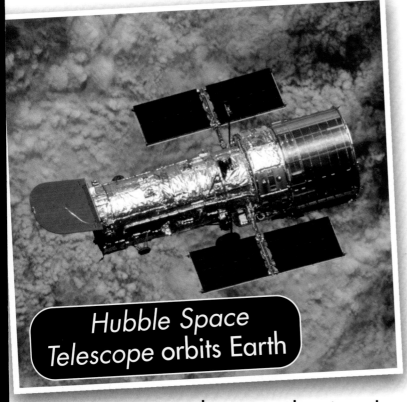

Hubble Space Telescope orbits Earth

The **Hubble Space Telescope**, launched in 1990, has since discovered at least another twelve small moons around Uranus!

Hubble can see Uranus's smallest moons. Some measure only 10 miles (16 km) across. They are all 3 billion miles (4.8 billion km) from Earth!

Uranus's Biggest Moons

Astronomers think Uranus's five biggest moons are made of ice and rock.

William Herschel discovered Uranus's two biggest moons, Oberon and Titania.

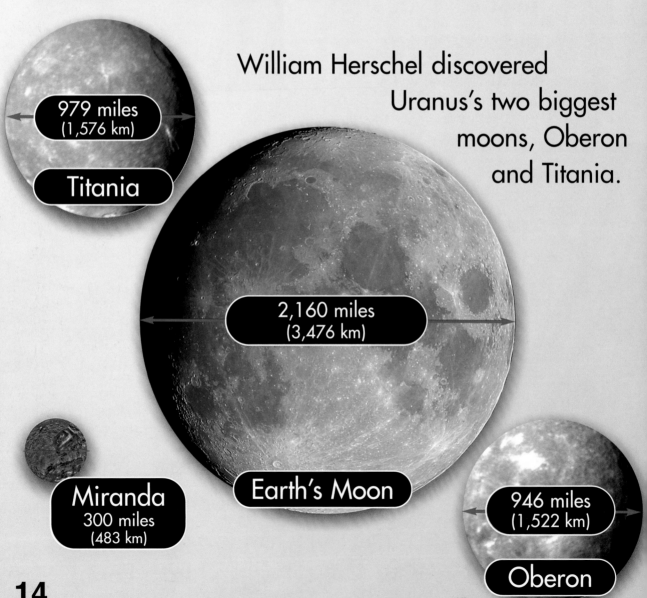

979 miles
(1,576 km)

Titania

2,160 miles
(3,476 km)

Miranda
300 miles
(483 km)

Earth's Moon

946 miles
(1,522 km)

Oberon

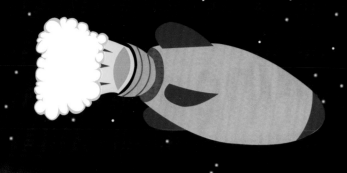

In 1986, *Voyager 2* took nine separate photographs of different sections of Miranda. A computer pieced them together to make one photograph.

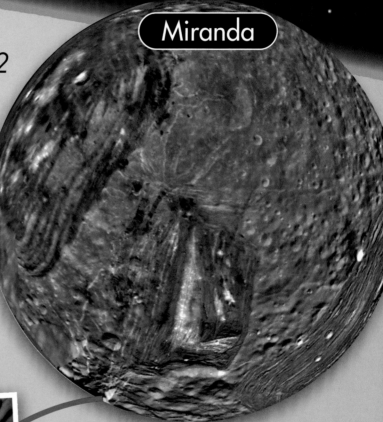

Miranda

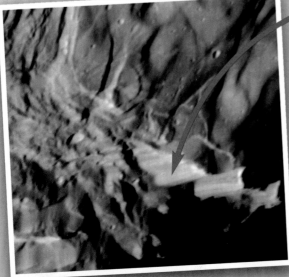

This **canyon** on Miranda is about 12 miles (20 km) deep. Earth's Grand Canyon is only about 1 mile (1.6 km) deep.

Uranus's Rings

Uranus has rings made of dust and rocks. Astronomers looking through telescopes discovered the rings in 1977.

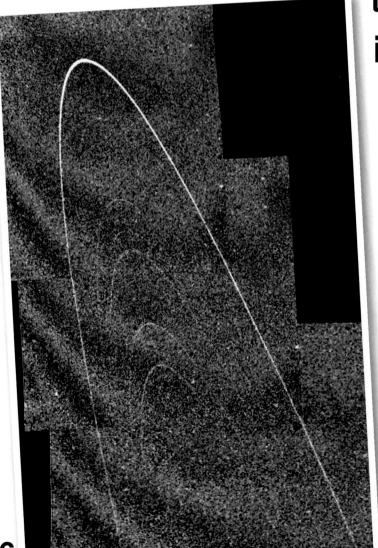

In 1986, *Voyager 2* found more rings around Uranus. We now know Uranus has at least eleven rings. You cannot see all eleven of the rings in this picture, which was taken by *Voyager 2*.

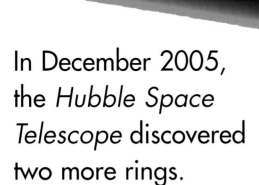

In December 2005, the *Hubble Space Telescope* discovered two more rings.

Astronomers think that when space rocks hit Uranus's moons, dust and stones break off and help form more rings around the planet.

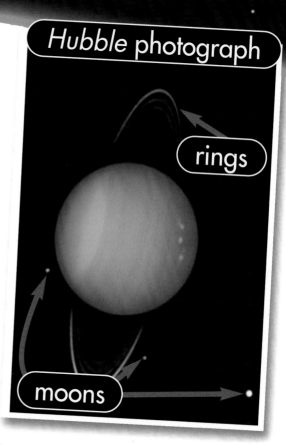

Hubble photograph

rings

moons

This painting shows how Uranus's rings might look close up.

17

What Can We See?

Uranus is difficult to study because it is so far from Earth. Astronomers use math in many ways to learn more about Uranus.

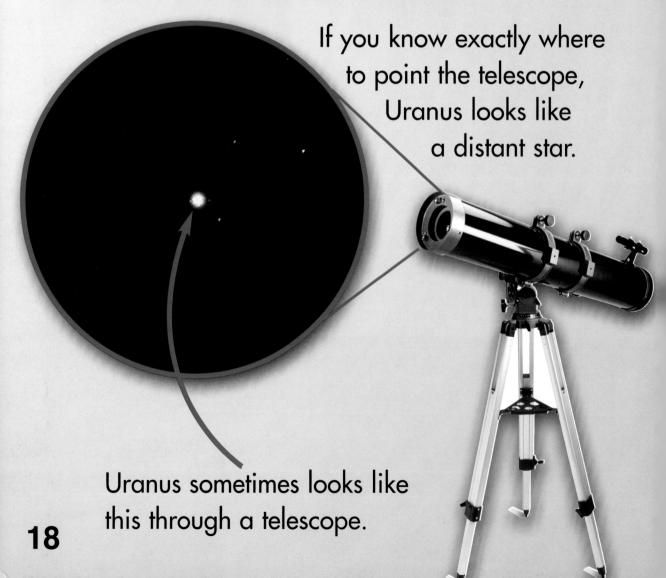

If you know exactly where to point the telescope, Uranus looks like a distant star.

Uranus sometimes looks like this through a telescope.

The *Hubble Space Telescope* takes the best photographs of Uranus.

Hubble photographs

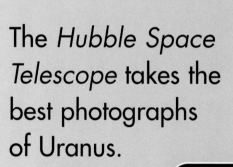

A computer added the red color to this picture. The whitish areas are clouds around Uranus.

Hubble orbits above Earth's atmosphere. It takes pictures that are much clearer than pictures taken by even the largest telescopes on Earth.

19

Missions to Uranus

Voyager 2 is the only space mission that ever visited Uranus. *Voyager 2* discovered some moons. It also discovered that Uranus's orbit is tilted.

Titan-Centaur rocket

TITAN/CENTAUR COMPL

Voyager 2 blasted into space aboard a Titan-Centaur rocket on August 20, 1977.

The rocket was launched from the Kennedy Space Center at Cape Canaveral, Florida.

Voyager 2 flew past Jupiter in 1979, past Saturn in 1981, and past Uranus in 1986.

a painting of *Voyager 2's* mission

In 1989, the space probe reached Neptune.
Voyager 2 is now at the edge of our solar system.
It should send information back to Earth until 2030. **21**

Future Missions

Astronomers are sure it is too cold for life on Uranus, but they would like to find out more about the planet. Right now, no new missions are planned.

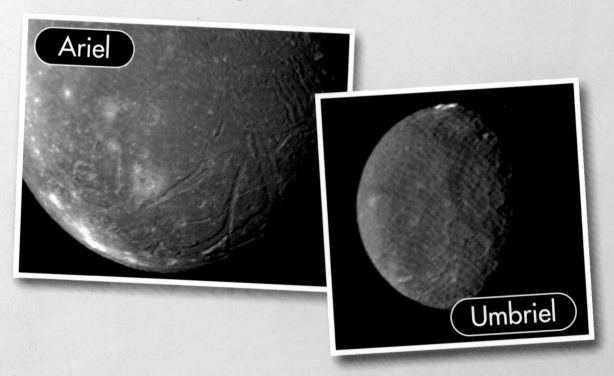

Ariel

Umbriel

Astronomers would like to take a closer look at Uranus's moons. They also think Uranus might have more moons to be discovered!

It takes nearly nine years to get from Earth to Uranus! Any new mission to Uranus will be carried out by **robots** instead of **astronauts**.

a painting of Uranus and its rings

Voyager 2 disk

Voyager 2 carries a special disk. The disk contains information and greetings from Earth. We do not know if any far-away planets have life-forms that could read the disk! What do you think?

23

Glossary

astronauts people trained to travel or work in space

astronomers people who study outer space, often using telescopes

atmosphere the gases that surround a planet, moon, or star

canyon a deep valley, often formed by water

Earth years the time it takes Earth to orbit the Sun once. One Earth year is 365 days long.

Hubble Space Telescope a telescope that studies space from high above Earth's atmosphere.

hydrogen gas a very light gas. The Sun is made mostly of hydrogen.

liquid something that has no shape of its own and flows easily.

methane gas a gas with no smell. It burns easily.

orbit the path that a space object takes around the Sun or a planet

robots machines that perform tasks for people

solar system the Sun and everything that is in orbit around it

space probe a spacecraft sent from Earth to explore the solar system

telescope an instrument used for studying objects that are very far away

year the time it takes a planet to orbit the Sun once

Index